Land

What processes created the Earth's landscapes and how does the land affect people?

GEOLOGY

Job description: The study of Earth's rocky parts and how they have changed over time.

Equipment: includes hammers, hard hat, sample bags, and mineral test kit.

VOLCANOLOGY

Job description: The study of volcanoes and their activity to predict if and when they will erupt.

Equipment: includes seismometers, satellite images, heat images, and gas sampling kit.

CARTOGRAPHY

Job description: The study of collecting information about an area and making maps, charts, and pictures.

Equipment: includes compass, global positioning system (GPS) receiver, levelling tools, and tape measure.

GEMOLOGY

Job description: The study of precious stones to grade and identify their quality and structure.

Equipment: includes microscope, jeweller's loupe for grading, and refractometer for identifying.

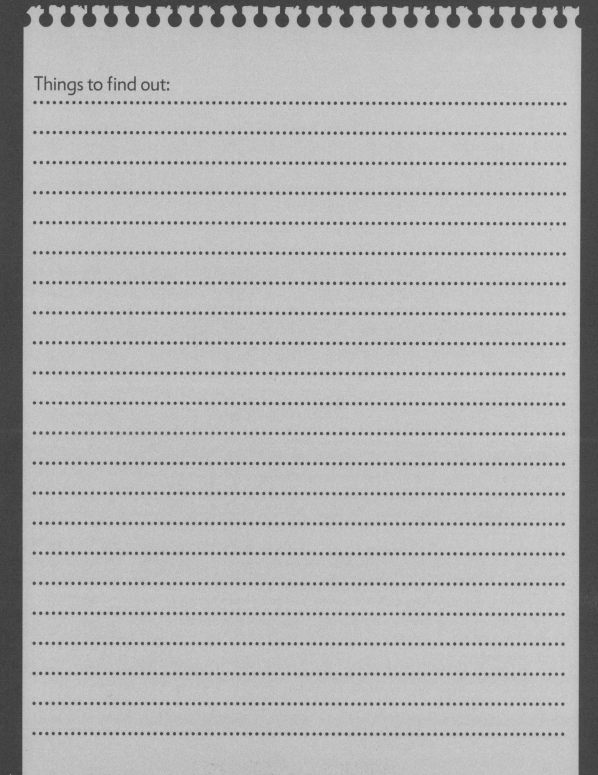

Things to find out:

DK findout!
Earth

Author and consultant: Maryam Sharif-Draper

Project editors Manisha Majithia, Ishani Nandi
Senior editor Cécile Landau
Editorial assistant Megan Weal
Senior art editor Clare Joyce
Project art editor Nehal Verma
Art editor Jaileen Kaur
Managing editors Deborah Lock,
Alka Thakur Hazarika
Managing art editors Vicky Short,
Romi Chakraborty
DTP designers Dheeraj Singh, Ashok Kumar
Picture researcher Nishwan Rasool
Pre-production producer Dragana Puvacic
Production controller Isabelle Schart
Art director Martin Wilson
Publisher Sarah Larter
Publishing director Sophie Mitchell
Educational consultant Jacqueline Harris

First published in Great Britain in 2017 by
Dorling Kindersley Limited
80 Strand, London, WC2R 0RL

Copyright © 2017 Dorling Kindersley Limited
A Penguin Random House Company
10 9 8 7 6 5 4 3 2 1
001-299033-Sept/2017

A CIP catalogue record for this book
is available from the British Library.
ISBN: 978-0-2412-8510-7

Printed and bound in China

A WORLD OF IDEAS:
SEE ALL THERE IS TO KNOW

www.dk.com

Contents

Meteor shower

Li River, Guilin, China

Satellite

Political globe of the world

Mauna Loa, Hawaii, USA

Tsunami wave

What is Earth?

Earth is our home. It is nearly 150 million km (94 million miles) from the Sun, and is the fifth-largest planet in our solar system. Earth is also the only planet in our solar system where water is found on the surface, which allows animals and plants to live there.

Day
In an area of the Earth that is facing the Sun, it will be light, and therefore day.

DAY

EQUATOR

Sun's rays
As the Sun's rays reach Earth, they provide light and warmth. Without the Sun, life on Earth would not exist.

Equator
This is an imaginary line around the middle of the Earth. It lies halfway between the North and South Poles.

! WOW!

Our Sun is huge – about **one million times bigger** than the Earth!

Solar system

Our solar system is made up of the Sun and the eight planets that travel around it – Mercury, Venus, Earth, Mars, Jupiter, Saturn, Uranus, and Neptune. The solar system also has moons, comets, asteroids, and meteoroids zipping through it. Scientists estimate that our solar system was formed about 4.6 billion years ago!

Mercury

Venus

Earth

Mars

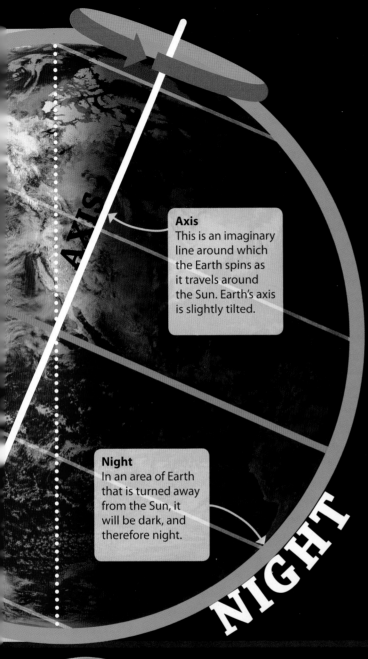

AXIS

Axis
This is an imaginary line around which the Earth spins as it travels around the Sun. Earth's axis is slightly tilted.

Night
In an area of Earth that is turned away from the Sun, it will be dark, and therefore night.

NIGHT

Earth's story

It is thought that Earth, and the other planets, formed as gravity forced material in clouds of gas and dust together, creating clumps of rock. These gradually grew bigger to form planets. Over time, the conditions on Earth evolved to support life.

Earth's orbit

This is the path that the Earth takes as it travels around the Sun. Earth's orbit does not form a perfect circle. It is a slightly flattened circle, or oval. Earth takes 365 days, or a whole year, to make one complete journey around the Sun.

The number of days it takes Earth to orbit the Sun

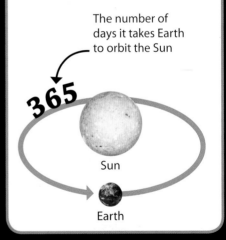

365

Sun

Earth

Jupiter

Saturn

Uranus

Neptune

Exosphere

This is the highest layer of Earth's atmosphere, where it merges into space. Only a few, very thin wisps of gas are found this high above our planet. It would be impossible to breathe here!

Satellites

These orbit Earth in the thermosphere and exosphere. We use them to make phone calls and watch TV. Scientists also use satellites to find out more about space.

Thermosphere

Unlike in other layers of Earth's atmosphere, temperatures here increase as you go higher, some parts rising to 2,000°C (3,600°F)! Satellites, including the International Space Station, orbit Earth in the thermosphere.

! **WOW!**

Without some of the gases in its atmosphere, Earth would be too cold to live on!

Aurora

These bright lights appear in the thermosphere when particles from the Sun fall into Earth's atmosphere.

Earth's atmosphere

Earth is surrounded by a thick layer of gases, called the atmosphere. These gases protect Earth from the Sun's rays, keeping temperatures on our planet at a comfortable level. Earth's atmosphere is divided into a number of distinct layers. At the outer edge of the atmosphere, there is no clear boundary. It just fades into space.

50-80 **16-50** **0-16**

Mesosphere

The top of the mesosphere is the coldest part of the Earth's atmosphere, with temperatures of -143°C (-226°F). Gases here are thick enough to slow down meteors, causing them to burn up.

Stratosphere

The air in this layer is very dry and still. The ozone layer, which protects plants and animals on Earth from dangerous ultraviolet (UV) rays that are given off by the Sun, lies in the stratosphere.

Troposphere

The gases found in the troposphere make up the air that we breathe. Therefore, life exists in this layer. Clouds form here, and it is where most of our weather occurs.

Meteors
These are bits of matter from outer space that burn up on entering Earth's atmosphere, creating streaks of light. They are also called shooting stars.

Sun's rays

Reflected rays

Weather balloons
Scientists launch these to collect information about conditions in Earth's atmosphere that affect the weather, such as temperature and air pressure.

Ozone layer
This thin band, running across the stratosphere, contains a large amount of ozone, a gas that absorbs ultraviolet (UV) rays from the Sun. UV rays cause sunburn, and can cause skin cancer.

Mountains
Some of Earth's highest mountains extend quite a way into the troposphere.

Planes
Planes usually fly in the troposphere, but may go up to the edge of the stratosphere.

7

Structure of the Earth

Planet Earth is made up of a number of different layers. Some of these are solid, while others are liquid or a mixture of both. Knowing about Earth's structure will help you understand what is happening on the surface – where you live.

Looking under the surface

If you could slice a section out of the Earth, you would see its different layers.

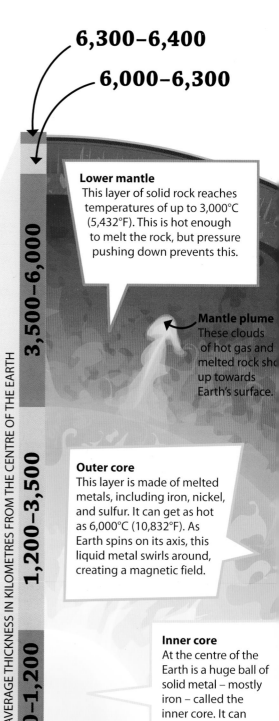

6,300–6,400

6,000–6,300

AVERAGE THICKNESS IN KILOMETRES FROM THE CENTRE OF THE EARTH

3,500–6,000

1,200–3,500

0–1,200

Lower mantle
This layer of solid rock reaches temperatures of up to 3,000°C (5,432°F). This is hot enough to melt the rock, but pressure pushing down prevents this.

Mantle plume
These clouds of hot gas and melted rock sho up towards Earth's surface.

Outer core
This layer is made of melted metals, including iron, nickel, and sulfur. It can get as hot as 6,000°C (10,832°F). As Earth spins on its axis, this liquid metal swirls around, creating a magnetic field.

Inner core
At the centre of the Earth is a huge ball of solid metal – mostly iron – called the inner core. It can reach temperatures of up to 5,500°C (10,000°F), as hot as the Sun's surface.

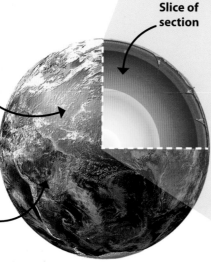

Slice of section

Water
Seas and oceans cover about 71 per cent of Earth's surface.

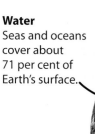

Land
Just 29 per cent of Earth's surface is land, which is split up into continents.

Inside and outside
Ocean and land cover Earth's surface, but inside are many complex layers.

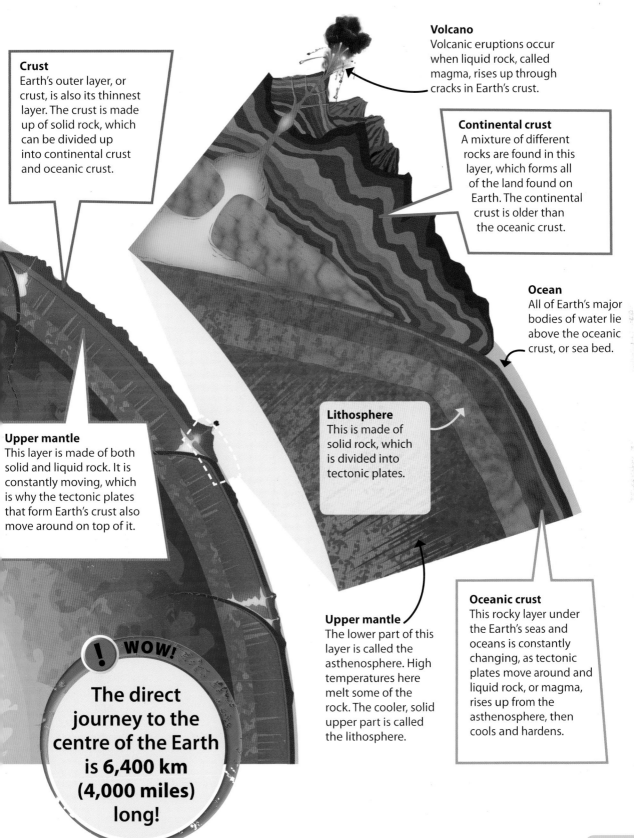

Crust
Earth's outer layer, or crust, is also its thinnest layer. The crust is made up of solid rock, which can be divided up into continental crust and oceanic crust.

Volcano
Volcanic eruptions occur when liquid rock, called magma, rises up through cracks in Earth's crust.

Continental crust
A mixture of different rocks are found in this layer, which forms all of the land found on Earth. The continental crust is older than the oceanic crust.

Ocean
All of Earth's major bodies of water lie above the oceanic crust, or sea bed.

Lithosphere
This is made of solid rock, which is divided into tectonic plates.

Upper mantle
This layer is made of both solid and liquid rock. It is constantly moving, which is why the tectonic plates that form Earth's crust also move around on top of it.

Upper mantle
The lower part of this layer is called the asthenosphere. High temperatures here melt some of the rock. The cooler, solid upper part is called the lithosphere.

Oceanic crust
This rocky layer under the Earth's seas and oceans is constantly changing, as tectonic plates move around and liquid rock, or magma, rises up from the asthenosphere, then cools and hardens.

! WOW!
The direct journey to the centre of the Earth is 6,400 km (4,000 miles) long!

Moving Earth

Earth's crust is divided up into large pieces called tectonic plates. These plates move around on the molten rock under them. Where the edges of these moving plates meet, the Earth's crust is unstable, and earthquakes and volcanic eruptions occur. Mountains may also form there.

KEY

All Earth's tectonic plates have names. The colour of the line along their edges tells you what type of boundary they have.

— **Convergent**

— **Divergent**

— **Transform**

Plate boundaries

These are where the edges of tectonic plates meet. There are three main types – convergent, divergent, and transform boundaries. They differ in how the plates involved meet.

Convergent boundary

Here, two plates move towards each other. They may push together, forming mountains. But, if one plate gets pushed under the other, a volcano can form.

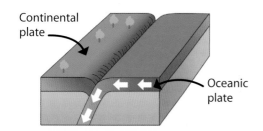

Continental plate

Oceanic plate

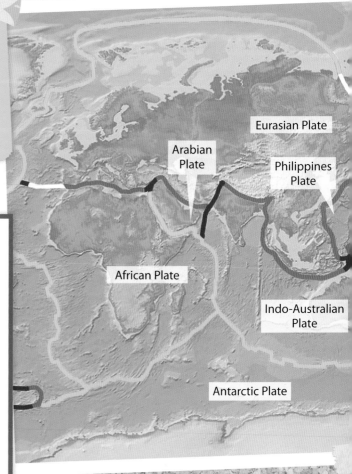

Eurasian Plate

Arabian Plate

Philippines Plate

African Plate

Indo-Australian Plate

Antarctic Plate

Ring of Fire

This area in the Pacific Ocean is one of the most unstable parts of the Earth's crust. Here, the tectonic plates move around a lot, causing some of the world's worst earthquakes. It is also where there are many active volcanoes.

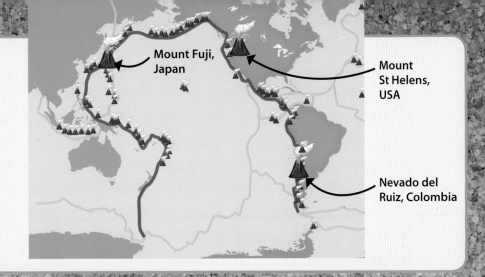

Mount Fuji, Japan

Mount St Helens, USA

Nevado del Ruiz, Colombia

North American Plate

Juan de Fuca Plate

Caribbean Plate

Cocos Plate

Pacific Plate

South American Plate

Nazca Plate

Scotia Plate

Transform boundary

When two plates rub against each other, this can cause an earthquake. They may slide by in opposite directions or move in the same direction at different speeds.

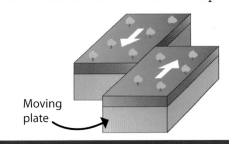

Moving plate

Divergent boundary

Here, plates move away from each other, and plate material forms in the gap left between them. When this happens under the ocean, new ocean floor is created.

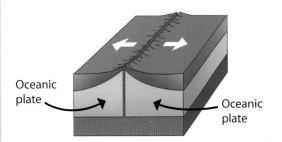

Oceanic plate

Oceanic plate

Mountains

Mountains are formed when the Earth's tectonic plates move and collide with one another. As the plates continue to move, magma and land may be pushed up, forming mountains.

Fault-block mountains

Cracks in the Earth's crust can create massive blocks of rock that then move apart. As they move, one block may slide under another, pushing it up. This leaves large blocks of rock sticking up, high above the Earth's surface. These are fault-block mountains.

FACT FILE

» **Name:** Sierra Nevada

» **Height:** 4,418 m (14,494 ft)

» **Location:** USA

Sierra Nevada MOUNTAINS

Dome mountains

When large amounts of the magma under the Earth's crust bubble up towards the surface, layers of rock above the magma are pushed up to form dome mountains. The inside of these mountains is filled with magma that has cooled and hardened.

GREETINGS FROM
Puy de Dôme

WISH YOU WERE HERE...
Himalayas

Fold mountains

These are the most common type of mountain. They form when two or more tectonic plates are pushed together, causing layers of rock on the seafloor to crumple and fold. Over millions of years, these folded layers are slowly pushed up higher to form mountains.

Volcanic mountains

A volcanic eruption occurs when magma bubbles up and eventually erupts through a crack in the Earth's crust. This causes molten rock, known as lava, to flow over the land, before it cools and hardens. Further eruptions create more layers of hardened lava, which build up to form a mountain.

MOUNT
Kilimanjaro

Volcanoes

Volcanoes form when magma – a mixture of hot gas, ash, and melted rock – erupts from a crack in the Earth's surface. The melted rock, called lava, flows out and hardens. As layers of lava build up, the volcano gets bigger. A volcano can be active, dormant, or extinct.

STRATOVOLCANO
Mount Fuji, Japan

Stratovolcanoes are tall and cone-shaped, with steep sides. They are made up of lots of layers of lava and ash that have cooled and hardened. Their eruptions can be very powerful and dangerous.

! WOW!

Most of Earth's **active** volcanoes lie hidden from view, under the ocean!

Inside a volcano

When pressure in the magma chamber under a volcano gets too high, the magma is forced up and out of the main vent. This is called an eruption. The force of this eruption blows rock off the top of the volcano, creating a bowl-shaped hollow, called a crater. In some volcanoes, magma also erupts from smaller vents that branch out from the main vent.

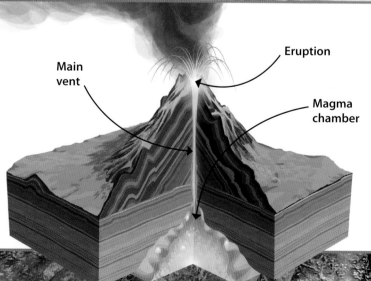

Main vent

Eruption

Magma chamber

SHIELD
Mauna Loa, Hawaii, USA

Shield volcanoes have gently sloping side and are formed from thin, runny lava. Their eruptions are less explosive and much less dangerous than other volcanoes. These gentle eruptions can continue for years.

CINDER CONE
Paricutin, Mexico

Cinder cone volcanoes are the smallest and most common type of volcano. They are cone-shaped with steep sides. Their eruptions are usually not too violent.

CALDERA
Ngorongoro, Tanzania

Calderas are large, circular hollows, almost like a bowl. They form when a massive eruption forces most of the magma out of the chamber under the volcano, causing it to collapse.

Earthquakes

When the rocky tectonic plates that form Earth's crust move suddenly, large waves of energy spread out, causing the ground to shake. This is an earthquake. Some earthquakes are fairly gentle and may even go unnoticed, but others can bring terrible destruction.

What causes an earthquake?

The plates in Earth's crust constantly slide past each other, but can get stuck. Pressure then builds up until the plates finally move, sending out shock waves. The focus of an earthquake is the point inside the ground where pressure builds up. The epicentre is the point on the surface above the focus.

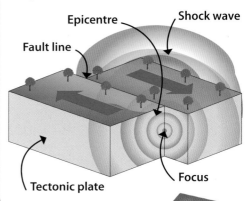

Epicentre

Shock wave

Fault line

Tectonic plate

Focus

Earthquake crack

An earthquake can cause large cracks to open up in the Earth's surface. Many are small, no more than a few metres deep or wide, but others are massive, and whole buildings can fall into them.

5–6

1–2

2.5–4

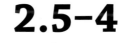

Seismograph

This machine is used to measure the force of the vibrations caused by an earthquake. It records how powerful these vibrations are on a numbered scale.

Mild tremors

Earthquakes that a seismograph records as having a force of 2.5–4 are felt as mild tremors. They cause little or no damage, although trees may sway and windows rattle.

Italy 2009

In 2009, an earthquake measuring 6.3 on a seismograph struck L'Aquila in central Italy. Many buildings collapsed and around 300 people died. Thousands of smaller earthquakes, called aftershocks, followed.

Sumatra 2004

This massive earthquake had a force of 9.3! It triggered a series of huge waves, called tsunamis, that travelled for thousands of kilometres across the Indian Ocean, killing 280,000 people.

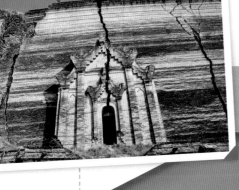

6.3

7.9

9.3

Wobbling dishes

When an earthquake has a force of 5–6, windows are likely to crack and dishes fall off shelves and smash. Some buildings may suffer serious damage.

China 2008

A force-8 earthquake struck Sichuan Province, China, in 2008. Huge chunks of rock fell down from the mountains, smashing towns and villages. Tremors were felt up to 1,700 km (1,060 miles) away.

Sahara Desert, Africa

Hot deserts
Temperatures often reach 50°C (122°F) or higher during the day in hot deserts. But at night, it can be very cold. Most hot deserts are near the equator, where there is strong sunlight all year round.

Atacama Desert, South America

Coastal deserts
Here, cold winds blowing off the ocean cause thick fog to form and drift inland. Water droplets in the fog soon dry up under the hot Sun, rather than falling as rain, leaving the land below very dry.

Deserts

About a third of Earth's surface is covered by deserts. They are areas that get little or no rain, so they are extremely dry. Only a few species of animals and plants can survive in them. We usually think of deserts as very hot places, but some are very cold.

! WOW!

The largest desert, the Sahara, covers about **a quarter** of Africa!

Cold deserts

The largest cold deserts are in Central Asia, usually in high, flat areas. They are very dry, like all deserts, but are also very cold for most of the time. During the long winters, temperatures often drop as low as -40°C (-40°F).

Gobi Desert, Central Asia

Ross Island, Antarctica

Polar deserts

These are extremely dry and cold. Temperatures rarely rise above 10°C (50°F), even in summer. Some are covered in ice and snow all year, while others are covered in gravel and large rocks. Most of Antarctica is polar desert.

Desert landforms

Over thousands of years, many different natural features, or landforms, have developed in deserts. These include hills; mountains; narrow, steep-sided valleys called canyons; large, flat areas called plains; sand dunes; strange rock formations; and oases.

Sand dunes
These hills are formed by the wind blowing across the desert sand, so that it piles up.

Oases
Rare underground water can create pools of water. Plants then spring up around them.

Mesas and buttes
Sand and grit, carried by the wind, wear away rock to create these steep, flat-topped hills.

Water

Water is essential to life on Earth. Without it, plants and animals would not be able to survive. Around 71 per cent of Earth is covered in water. This includes both salt water and fresh water. Not all of Earth's water is easily available for us to use.

29%
LAND

71%
WATER

SALT WATER

97.5%

FRESH WATER

0.3%
Only a small part of Earth's fresh water is found in lakes and rivers. We use it for washing and drinking.

30.8%
Some fresh water lies under Earth's surface. This groundwater flows into lakes and rivers, so we also use it in our daily lives

68.9%
This portion of Earth's fresh water is found in ice caps and glaciers. It is therefore very difficult for us to access and use.

Water on Earth

Most of Earth's water – 97.5 per cent of it – is salt water that makes up the oceans and seas. The 2.5 per cent that is left is fresh water. This is found in ice caps, glaciers, lakes, rivers, and sometimes underground.

The water cycle

Earth's water is always moving from one place to another. This process, called the water cycle, is a continuous journey, in which water moves between the land, the atmosphere, and the ocean.

The Sun's heat makes water evaporate, or turn to vapour, which rises into the air.

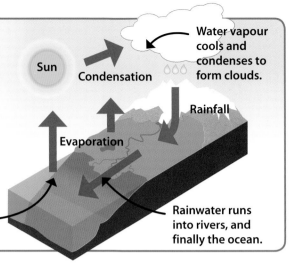

Sun

Condensation

Water vapour cools and condenses to form clouds.

Rainfall

Evaporation

Rainwater runs into rivers, and finally the ocean.

How we use water

We use large quantities of water. We drink it, wash with it, use it in industry, and also prepare food with it. Below are the percentages of the water that each person uses every day for these activities.

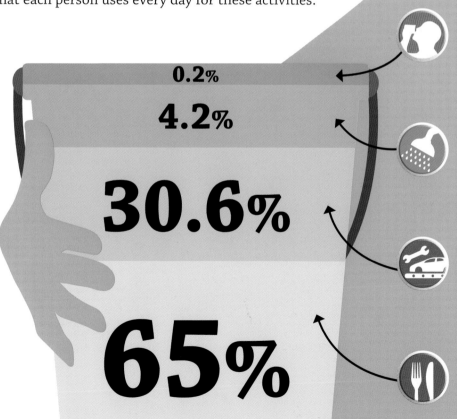

0.2%

4.2%

30.6%

65%

Drinking
Only a small amount of the water a person uses every day is for drinking.

Personal
Washing, cleaning your teeth, and flushing the toilet use up this share.

Manufactured goods
Nearly a third of each person's daily water is used to make things. This includes items such as televisions and phones.

Food production
This takes up most of the water we use. Water is an essential part of our diet. Without it, our bodies would not work!

Oceans

Around 71 per cent of the Earth's surface is covered by oceans. Many different and interesting features are found in and around them, and a huge variety of animals and plants have adapted to life in this watery world.

Pacific green turtle

Nishinoshima volcanic island, Japan

Volcanic islands
These islands are formed from layers of magma, or hot liquid rock, which erupts from a volcano under the water, then cools and hardens. The magma layers eventually build up to create an island.

Open ocean
This is the top layer of the ocean, nearest the surface. The open ocean is vast. Although food can sometimes be hard to find, many animals, such as dolphins, seals, and turtles, live there.

Oceanic trench
When tectonic plates in the ocean floor move and collide, one may be pushed under the other, creating a narrow trench. These trenches are the deepest places in the Earth's oceans.

Seamounts
These underwater mountains are formed by volcanic eruptions on the ocean floor. Most of them are not erupting.

Tectonic plates in the ocean floor are moving.

Tectonic plates in the ocean floor are moving.

Mupe Bay, Jurassic Coast, Dorset, UK

Great Barrier Reef, Australia

Coral reefs
These are made from the skeletons left by tiny sea animals, called coral polyps, when they die. The skeletons build up into huge reefs, where plants and other sea creatures live.

Rock pools
When the tide goes out on a rocky seashore, pools of water are left behind in holes in the rocks. These then become home to a huge range of plants and animals, such as shellfish and sea anemones.

Oceanic ridge
Moving tectonic plates can also create underwater mountains. The Mid-Atlantic Ridge, under the Atlantic Ocean, is more than 64,000 km (40,000 miles) long.

Hydrothermal vents
When sea water filters down cracks in the Earth's crust, it is heated by volcanic activity. Hot water then spurts out through the cracks or vents.

! WOW!

Nearly **95%** of the world's oceans remain unexplored!

Rivers

A river is a natural channel of fresh water that flows across the Earth's surface. All rivers start in mountains or hills and flow down towards the sea or ocean, or into another large area of water. They may be short or flow for hundreds of kilometres.

Source
This is where a river starts, high up in the mountains. The source, or place where the river starts from, could be a spring or a lake, or even a melting glacier. A river can have more than one source.

Iguazu Falls, Argentina, South America

Waterfall
Rivers usually flow over a mixture of hard and soft rock. The force of the water will wear away more soft rock than harder rock. Where this happens, there may be a steep drop in the level of the riverbed, creating a waterfall.

Tributary
A stream or river that flows into a larger river, rather than directly to the sea, is called a tributary. Some large rivers have hundreds of tributaries!

V-shaped valley and gorge
Near its source, a river flows very fast. The rushing water wears away the surrounding rock. This widens and deepens the river channel, forming a gorge or V-shaped valley.

Fast-flowing

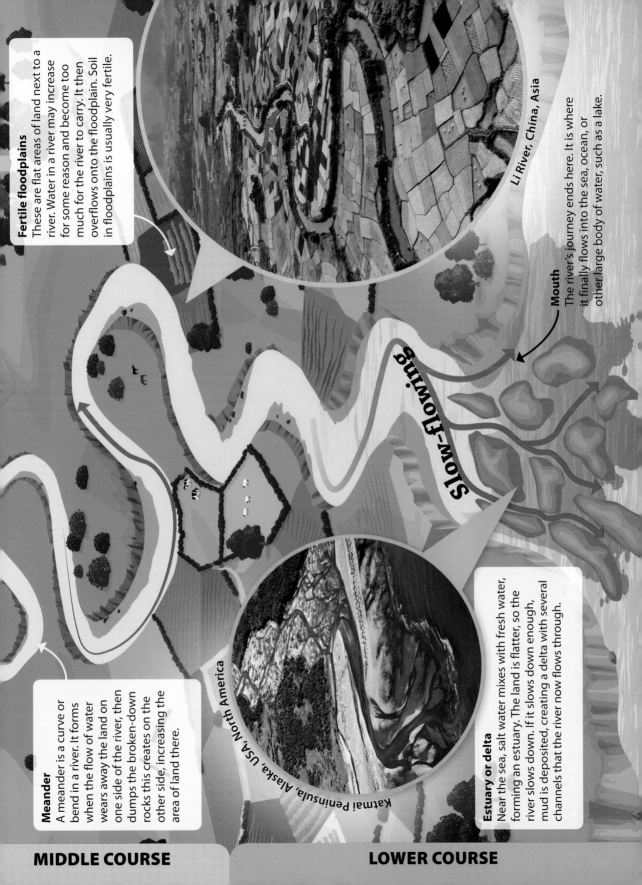

Fertile floodplains

These are flat areas of land next to a river. Water in a river may increase for some reason and become too much for the river to carry. It then overflows onto the floodplain. Soil in floodplains is usually very fertile.

Li River, China, Asia

Mouth
The river's journey ends here. It is where it finally flows into the sea, ocean, or other large body of water, such as a lake.

Slow-flowing

Meander
A meander is a curve or bend in a river. It forms when the flow of water wears away the land on one side of the river, then dumps the broken-down rocks this creates on the other side, increasing the area of land there.

Katmai Peninsula, Alaska, USA, North America

Estuary or delta
Near the sea, salt water mixes with fresh water, forming an estuary. The land is flatter, so the river slows down. If it slows down enough, mud is deposited, creating a delta with several channels that the river now flows through.

MIDDLE COURSE

LOWER COURSE

Glaciers

A glacier is a huge river of ice that forms when thick layers of snow fall on top of each other and are pressed together. Most glaciers form high up in mountains, where it's so cold that any snowfall never melts. They are found all around the world, usually in polar and mountainous regions.

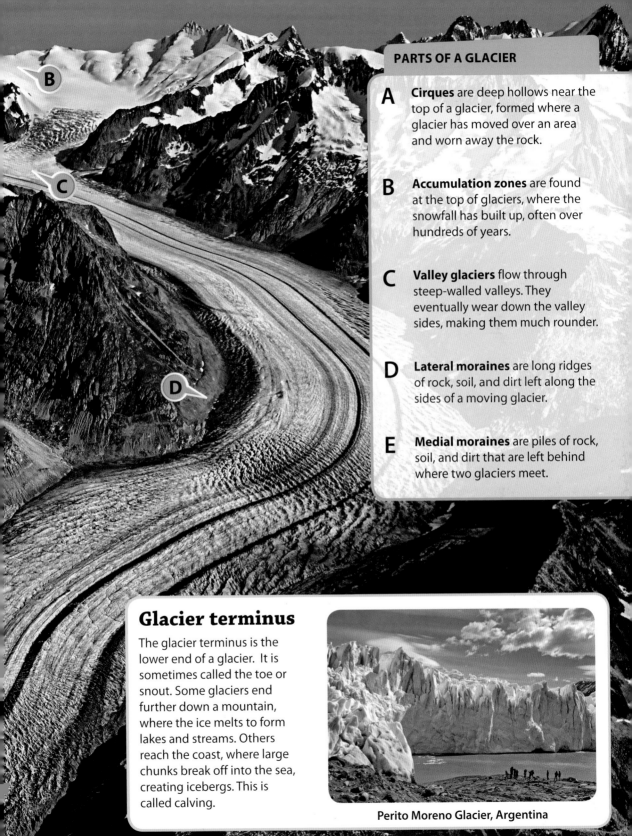

A **Cirques** are deep hollows near the top of a glacier, formed where a glacier has moved over an area and worn away the rock.

B **Accumulation zones** are found at the top of glaciers, where the snowfall has built up, often over hundreds of years.

C **Valley glaciers** flow through steep-walled valleys. They eventually wear down the valley sides, making them much rounder.

D **Lateral moraines** are long ridges of rock, soil, and dirt left along the sides of a moving glacier.

E **Medial moraines** are piles of rock, soil, and dirt that are left behind where two glaciers meet.

Glacier terminus

The glacier terminus is the lower end of a glacier. It is sometimes called the toe or snout. Some glaciers end further down a mountain, where the ice melts to form lakes and streams. Others reach the coast, where large chunks break off into the sea, creating icebergs. This is called calving.

Perito Moreno Glacier, Argentina

Erosion

Erosion is the wearing away of rocks and other matter on the Earth's surface by a natural force, such as a sliding glacier, a flowing river, or the wind. Material that is rubbed off is carried away and deposited somewhere else.

Water erosion
This is caused by falling rain or flowing water. Rivers, for example, wear away the land that they flow over, changing the surrounding landscape.

Wind erosion
The force of the wind can remove pieces of rock and carry them off. Wind erosion is common in deserts.

Ice erosion
As glaciers move, they rub away the land under them, carrying the broken-down material with them.

Coastal erosion
Crashing waves gradually wear away the rock in cliffs, and sweep up material from the beach.

This is when plants or animals cause rocks to break up. Plant roots often grow into small cracks in rocks, splitting them apart. An animal digging can also turn rocks into rubble.

Weathering

Weathering occurs when rocks are weakened, so that they crack and then break up into smaller pieces. This natural process can be caused by rainfall, changes in temperature, or even by plants as they grow. There are three types of weathering – biological, chemical, and physical.

! WOW!

Water erosion created the **Grand Canyon** in North America!

Chemical weathering
Chemical reactions can break up rock. Acid rain, for example, destroys the stone in statues and buildings.

Physical weathering
Wind, water, and temperature changes weaken rock. If water in a crack freezes, it expands and can tear a rock apart.

Caves

Caves are underground spaces or holes that are large enough for someone to enter. They form in many different ways, but mostly because of rock in the Earth's surface being worn away or crumbling. Caves usually have lots of interesting and exciting features to explore.

Stalagmite
Water dripping onto the cave floor leaves behind tiny rocky particles that were dissolved in it. As the dripping continues, these particles can build up to form a pillar of rock, or stalagmite.

Solutional caves
These are the most common type of cave. They are created when a build up of acidic water dissolves the rock around it. Holes and tunnels start to appear, getting bigger and bigger as more rock dissolves and is washed away.

Types of cave

Caves are found all over our planet. Some are small, single spaces, but others contain many chambers, linked by tunnels to form a huge maze of different areas. Although most caves are found in rock, some form in ice or lava.

Thurston cave, Hawaii, USA

Lava caves
When lava flows slowly over land around a volcano, it can harden on the surface, leaving liquid lava flowing underneath. This liquid drains away, leaving a hollow tube of rock that forms a cave.

Stalactite
These hang down like icicles. They form in the same way as stalagmites, from rocky particles dissolved in water, this time dripping from the cave's ceiling.

Soda straws
These thin, hollow tubes also form from dissolved particles in water, dripping slowly through the roof of a cave. They may grow into stalactites if the water keeps dripping for a very long time.

Column
If a stalagmite and stalactite become long enough and meet, they will form a rocky column. Columns are also created when a stalactite grows down to touch the cave floor.

Skaftafell cave, Iceland

Benagil cave, Portugal

Ice caves
Ice melting on top of a glacier can form a stream or waterfall that flows through the glacier. Eventually, this flowing water will hollow out part of the glacier, creating an ice cave.

Sea caves
These are formed by waves constantly battering against cliffs along the seashore. This leads to cracks appearing in the cliffs that get larger as beating waves continue to wear away the rock.

Record breakers

Our planet is full of incredible natural wonders, some of which are millions of years old. From skyscraping mountains to underground caves, here are five of Earth's record-breaking land features.

HIGHEST

Mount Everest, Nepal

The peak of Mount Everest lies 8,848 m (29,029 ft) above sea level, making it the world's highest mountain. It is ten times taller than the world's tallest building – the Burj Khalifa skyscraper in Dubai.

LONGEST

Nile River, Africa

The world's longest river is the Nile, at 6,825 km (4,238 miles) in length. It flows through 11 African countries, from Burundi to Egypt, where it meets the Mediterranean Sea. The Nile takes its name from the Greek for "river valley".

Krubera Cave, Georgia

The world's deepest cave lies in Asia. Stretching down 2,197 m (7,208 ft), it is nearly as deep as seven of Paris's Eiffel Towers. Russians call the cave *Voronya*, meaning "crow's cave", after the many crows nesting at the entrance.

Atacama Desert, Chile

Covering 1,000 km (600 miles), this South American desert is one of the driest places on Earth. Some parts have not seen rainfall since records began at least 400 years ago!

Angel Falls, Venezuela

Spectacular Angel Falls is the world's tallest waterfall. With a drop of 979 m (3,212 ft), it is more than twice the height of New York's Empire State Building. American pilot Jimmy Angel first spotted the waterfall from the air in 1933.

Biomes

Earth can be divided up into a number of different types of landscape. These zones are called biomes. Every biome is home to a particular group of plants and animals that are suited to the conditions found there.

MOUNTAINS

Mountains are high places with a cold, windy climate. It gets colder the higher up you go, so different groups of plants and animals are found at different heights.

Deserts

Deserts are very dry, as there is little or no rainfall. They can be very hot or very cold. The plants and animals found in deserts have adapted to living in these extreme conditions.

Rainforests

Rainforests get a lot of rain. Most of them also get a lot of sunlight, and are very hot all year round. They are home to many different plants and animals. The largest rainforest is the tropical Amazon rainforest in South America.

Wetlands

Wetlands are permanently flooded with water. This can be salt water, fresh water, or a mixture of both. Swamps, bogs, marshes, and deltas are all types of wetlands. Many birds thrive in this environment.

Coniferous forests

These forests have long, cold, snowy winters and short, warm summers. Trees here have adapted to this harsh climate. They are mostly evergreen, meaning they stay green all year round.

Deciduous forests

The temperature and rainfall in deciduous forests changes from season to season. During the autumn and winter, most trees change colour and lose their leaves.

GRASSLANDS

Grasslands get little rainfall. Only grass and a few small trees and bushes can grow in these dry places. But many animals, such as zebras and elephants, manage to live there.

TUNDRA

It is usually very cold and windy in the tundra, and there is not much rain. The ground is often covered in snow, so only a few plants and animals can live there.

Polar ice

This is the coldest biome on Earth. The freezing temperatures make it difficult for any plants to survive. Animals, such as polar bears, penguins, and seals, have adapted well to life here.

Conservation

We need to preserve and take good care of the Earth and its resources – the air, water, soil, plants, and animals on which we depend. This is what conservation is all about.

Learn to conserve!

START

Play this game to find out more about what can harm and what can help conserve our planet. Grab a dice and some counters, and get started!

How is our planet affected?

When people fail to conserve resources, Earth is affected in a number of ways:

Energy
Natural fuels, such as gas and coal, are used up too quickly, and cannot be replaced.

Pollution
Waste gases in the atmosphere trap heat from the Sun, so the Earth gets hotter.

Water
Higher temperatures, along with low rainfall, will eventually lead to drought.

Food
Drought and soil pollution can damage crops, so there is not enough food.

Forests
Cutting down trees can lead to plants and animals losing their homes.

Waste
Waste pollutes the environment. Also, if we waste resources, they will run out!

1 Tap left running. Miss a go!
Water is valuable. It is essential for life, so never waste it.

2

3 Saving paper. Move forward 3 places!
If you re-use scrap paper, and buy goods made from recycled paper, fewer trees will have to be cut down to make more paper.

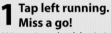

4 Driving to a friend's house. Miss a go!
Harmful gases from cars pollute the air. Walk or cycle instead.

9

8 Wind farm. Move forward 2 places!
A wind farm creates electricity. Wind is a renewable source of energy, so using it does not harm the environment.

7

6 Not recycling. Miss a go!
You are sending too much waste to landfill sites. This can damage the soil, water sources, and the atmosphere.

5

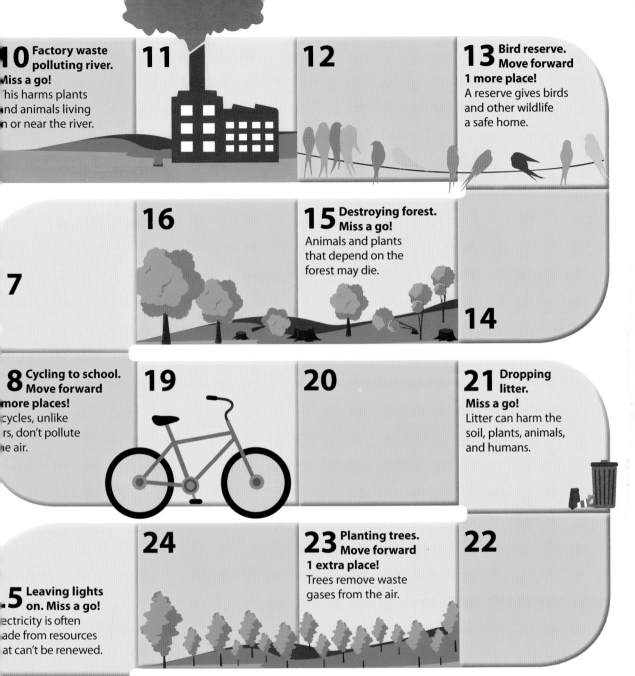

10 Factory waste polluting river. Miss a go!
This harms plants and animals living in or near the river.

11

12

13 Bird reserve. Move forward 1 more place!
A reserve gives birds and other wildlife a safe home.

16

15 Destroying forest. Miss a go!
Animals and plants that depend on the forest may die.

7

14

8 Cycling to school. Move forward more places!
Cycles, unlike cars, don't pollute the air.

19

20

21 Dropping litter. Miss a go!
Litter can harm the soil, plants, animals, and humans.

24

23 Planting trees. Move forward 1 extra place!
Trees remove waste gases from the air.

22

5 Leaving lights on. Miss a go!
Electricity is often made from resources that can't be renewed.

26 Growing fruit and vegetables. Move forward to finish!
Growing your own food saves on the cost of getting it to the shops.

27

You're a conservation expert!
Congratulations! You now know much more about how you can help make Earth a healthy and happy place. Spread the word – tell your family and friends, so they can help too.

FINISH

Sunshine
Heat from the Sun warms up the air, creating dry, bright weather conditions.

Wind
The Sun warms the air to different levels in different places. As warm air rises, cooler air rushes in to replace it, creating wind.

Clouds
Sunlight warms water in lakes and rivers, turning it into vapour that rises, and then forms tiny water droplets that gather together as clouds.

Weather

Sunshine, clouds, wind, rain, frost, and snow are some of the different weather conditions that we experience on Earth. The Sun plays a major role in the way one set of weather conditions changes to another set.

! WOW!

Large raindrops can fall to Earth at speeds of up to **32 km/h (20 mph)**!

Rain
Water droplets in clouds get bigger and become too heavy to remain in the sky. They then fall as rain.

Snow
When it gets very cold, water droplets in clouds form ice crystals that group together and fall as snowflakes.

Extreme weather

We say that we have extreme weather when conditions are very different to those that we are used to. Extreme weather can suddenly appear without warning, and may last for hours or even days, bringing death and destruction to an area. Flooding, heatwaves, blizzards, hurricanes, and tornadoes are all types of extreme weather.

Hurricane Felix, Honduras

Seasons and climate

Earth takes a year to travel, or orbit, around the Sun. At the same time, it spins on its axis, an imaginary line between the Poles. This means the amount of sunlight falling on any area of Earth varies during the year, changing the weather and creating seasons – spring, summer, autumn, and winter.

How seasons change

Earth tilts on its axis as it spins and orbits around the Sun. This tilt causes one half, or hemisphere, of Earth to lean towards the Sun, while the other half leans away. In the half leaning towards the Sun, it is summer. In the other half, it will then be winter.

SPRING

Spring is a time of change between summer and winter. Days gradually get brighter, warmer, and wetter. Leaves start to grow on the trees and baby animals are born.

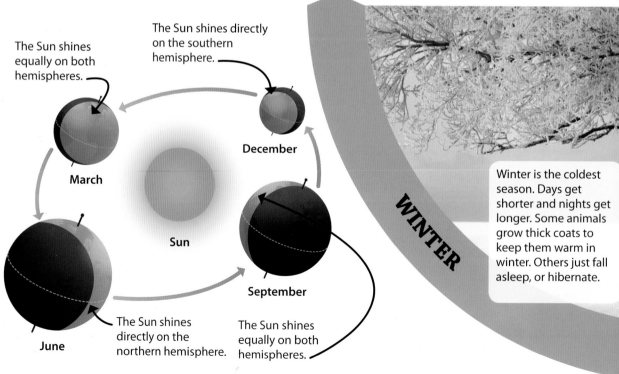

The Sun shines equally on both hemispheres.

The Sun shines directly on the southern hemisphere.

December

March

Sun

September

June

The Sun shines directly on the northern hemisphere.

The Sun shines equally on both hemispheres.

WINTER

Winter is the coldest season. Days get shorter and nights get longer. Some animals grow thick coats to keep them warm in winter. Others just fall asleep, or hibernate.

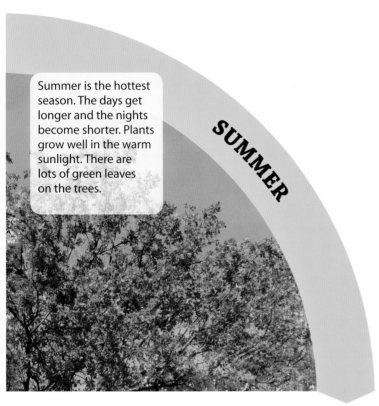

Summer is the hottest season. The days get longer and the nights become shorter. Plants grow well in the warm sunlight. There are lots of green leaves on the trees.

SUMMER

Autumn is when summer gradually changes into winter. Temperatures start to cool. The leaves on the trees change colour to orange and brown, then fall to the ground.

AUTUMN

Climate

The climate of an area is the type of weather it usually experiences. It includes the amount of rainfall, hours of sunshine, and highest, lowest, and average temperatures. Earth is divided into climate zones that are based on their distance from the equator.

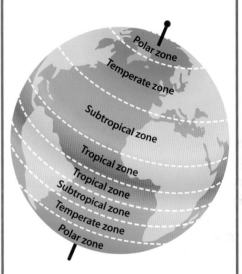

Polar zone
Temperate zone
Subtropical zone
Tropical zone
Tropical zone
Subtropical zone
Temperate zone
Polar zone

 Tropical zone This area is very hot and damp all year round. It rains a lot and thunderstorms are common.

 Subtropical zone Here, summers are long, dry, and hot. Winters are wet, but usually short and mild.

 Temperate zone Extreme conditions are rare here. Summers are warm and winters cold, but not freezing.

 Polar zone It is icy and dry all year round here. Winters are long and dark, while in summer the Sun shines most of the time.

Climate change

Earth's climate has always changed naturally over time. However, climate change now appears to be speeding up! Many recent changes in climate are caused by our modern way of life. Earth is getting warmer, which can have a huge effect on the environment.

Causes

Humans are thought to be responsible for the most recent, major climate changes. Waste gases from industry, transport, and deforestation have built up in Earth's atmosphere. These trap more heat around the Earth, so temperatures rise.

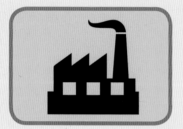

Industry

Whenever we burn oil, coal, or natural gas, waste gases are released into the atmosphere.

Transport

We now use cars, buses, and planes regularly. They all fill the air with lots of waste gases.

Deforestation

Trees help remove gases from the air. As more trees are cut down, more waste gases stay in the air.

How can we help?

There are many ways you can help slow down climate change. Just by turning off your computer or the TV when you're not using them, or the lights when you leave a room, or by walking to school, you reduce the level of waste gases in the atmosphere.

1 Renewable energy

Use more energy from resources that there are plenty of, such as sunshine, wind, and waves.

2 Green transport

Avoid transport that releases waste gases into the air. When you can, cycle or walk instead.

Effects

Extreme weather

Heatwaves, droughts, heavy rain, and flooding are becoming more and more common, because of Earth's atmosphere warming up.

Rise in sea levels

Higher temperatures melt glaciers and ice caps. The water formed eventually flows into the ocean. Sea levels rise and areas near the coast are flooded.

Changing natural habitats

Many animals live in special places, such as on sea ice or in coral reefs. Warmer temperatures can destroy both of these, so animals lose their home.

3

Recycle

Recycle plastic, glass, and paper. This reduces the amount of waste sent to landfill sites.

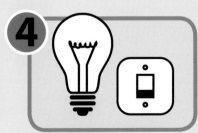

4

Save electricity

Stop leaving your computer or the TV on standby, and turn off lights when you leave a room.

5

Grow your own food

Food grown at or nearer home saves on the fuel needed to transport it to local shops.

Soil

Soil is the layer of loose material between the surface and the solid rock below the ground. Nothing can grow on Earth without it, but the soil varies in different places.

Grasses
The soil is rich in nutrients, so many grasses can grow healthily and quickly.

Leafcutter ants
Ants dig tunnels into the soil, letting in air and moving around decaying plants and animals, which adds nutrients to the soil.

Forest floor
Many leaves from the thick tree canopy fall to the dark forest floor and decay.

Long roots
Trees and grasses have long roots that go deep down to collect as much water as possible from the soil.

Dung beetle
These creatures feed on and break up, or decompose, animal poo, adding nutrients to the soil.

Buttress roots
Trees have shallow roots underground to quickly take in the water and nutrients in the topsoil.

Grassland

The soil is usually deep and full of nutrients. This is because rotting grass roots help to hold the soil together and add nutrients for new plants. Plants compete for water.

Tropical rainforest

The soil is very wet and many plants grow, so there is lots of humus to add nutrients to the soil. However, these nutrients are washed away by the constant rain, leaving shallow, acidic soil.

Soil profiles

Soil is made up of broken rocks, minerals, decaying plants and animals, tiny creatures, gases, and water. If a section is cut through soil, you will see many layers. The depth of the layers vary in different soils.

Humus
Dead plants and animals decay, adding nutrients, or goodness, to the soil.

Subsoil
This moist layer contains clay and minerals from the weathered rock.

Top soil This dark layer is full of tiny creatures and nutrients, which plants use to grow.

Leaching layer
Water drips through this layer, leaving mostly sand and silt.

Weathered rock
Large rocks are broken up from the solid bedrock below.

Cactus
Cacti have shallow roots and thick stems, so they can collect and store water.

Autumn leaves
When leaves drop to the forest floor, they decay, putting nutrients back into the soil.

Deep roots
Desert trees have very long roots to reach down and collect water from deep underground.

Earthworm
Burrowing earthworms mix the soil layers, letting air in and allowing water to drain through.

Tree roots
Roots of deciduous trees reach different layers of the soil to collect water and nutrients.

Kangaroo rat
When burrowing, animals break down large rocks, mix up the soil, and let air into it.

Temperate deciduous forest

The soil is moist and full of nutrients from decaying plants and animals, especially in autumn. The deep roots of plants break up the bedrock, which adds minerals. Water often drains through steadily.

Desert

The soil is very dry and few plants grow, so there is little humus. It is made up of boulders, pebbles, and sand, and is blown around by the wind. Any water drains through the sand easily.

Rock cycle

Rocks go through many changes over time. These are caused by different processes, such as heating, cooling, and weathering. The sequence of changes is called the rock cycle.

Cooling
When melted rock cools and hardens, it forms igneous rock. This can happen after a volcanic eruption or underground.

Igneous rock

Uplift
Metamorphic rock is forced upwards slowly by pressure and the movement of Earth's crust to form mountains.

Metamorphic rock

Heat and pressure
Some sedimentary rock is dragged down into the Earth's mantle, where pressure and heat changes the rock into metamorphic rock.

Melting
In the heat, some rocks melt into liquid, called magma. Pressure can force magma out of the ground.

Types of rocks

There are three different groups of rock: igneous, sedimentary, and metamorphic. Rocks are classified into these three different groups, depending on how they were formed.

Igneous rock
Types of igneous rock include basalt (shown here) and granite. These are formed by volcanic eruptions.

Sedimentary rock
Types of sedimentary rock include sandstone (shown here), chalk, and limestone. These form in layers of tiny rock pieces.

Metamorphic rock
Types of metamorphic rock include marble (shown here), slate, and shale. These are formed by heat and pressure.

Rocks on the move

Movements in the Earth's crust are causing rocks to slowly change. Volcanoes erupt and mountains are pushed upwards, and the rocks that come to the surface are broken down by weathering. This rock is moved and dragged down into the Earth's crust again.

Weathering and erosion
Rocks on the surface are broken down into smaller pieces by weathering. Erosion breaks down the rocks further.

Transportation and deposition
Pieces of broken rock, called sediment, are moved along by wind or water, and eventually end up in lakes and oceans.

Sedimentation and cementation
In lakes and oceans, layers of broken rock, dead plants, and animal remains build up and stick together. This makes sedimentary rock.

Sedimentary rock

Rock uses

Rocks and minerals make up much of our planet. They are formed deep inside the Earth over millions of years. Rocks exist in lots of different shapes, textures, and colours. They are mined to provide many of the things around us. Can you guess which rock is used where?

B Beaded necklace

A Steel nuts and bolts

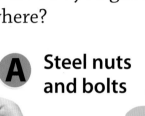

Iron ore
Ores are rocks in Earth's crust that contain metal. Iron is strong and hard, yet easy to work. It is often turned into steel.

1

Granite
Granite is formed deep inside Earth's crust, when magma cools down slowly. It is a tough rock, used in buildings and other large structures.

2

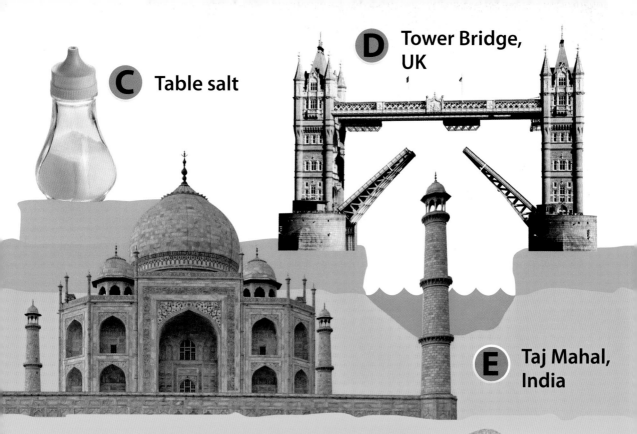

C Table salt

D Tower Bridge, UK

E Taj Mahal, India

3 Turquoise
This semi-precious stone is a mix of the metals copper and aluminium. Blue in colour, turquoise has been made into jewellery and sculptures for thousands of years.

5 Marble
Marble is actually made from the rock limestone. Strong heat and pressure can crystallize limestone and turn it into marble. It is easy to carve and polish, producing a very smooth finish. It is commonly used for sculptures and buildings.

Rock salt
Rock salt, also called halite, forms when sea water evaporates. It leaves behind salt crystals, which people can use to flavour food.

4

New York, USA

North America
This is the third-largest continent, and has the fourth-largest population. North America runs from the Arctic down to the equator, so the climate varies a lot.

South America
Many different types of weather and landscape are found in South America. Because of this, a huge variety of plants and animals live there. It is also home to the biggest rainforest in the world – the Amazon.

Amazon rainforest, Brazil

Continents

All of the land on Earth is divided up into seven large areas, called continents. These are North America, South America, Europe, Africa, Asia, Australia, and Antarctica. Each continent is divided up again into a number of different countries.

Antarctica
This is the coldest, driest, and windiest continent on Earth. It is almost entirely covered in ice for most of the year. Only a few species of animals and plants can live there.

South Georgi
Antarctica

me, Italy

FACT FILE

» **Land area:**
10.18 million sq km
(3.93 million sq miles)

» **Countries:** 50

» **Population:**
743.1 million

» **Largest city:**
Istanbul

Europe

Although Europe is the second-smallest continent, it has the world's third-largest population. The world's smallest country, Vatican City, is in Europe.

Beijing, China

FACT FILE

» **Land area:**
44.58 million sq km
(17.21 million sq miles)

» **Countries:** 48

» **Population:**
4.44 billion

» **Largest city:**
Tokyo

Asia

This is the world's largest continent. It also has the largest population and contains the world's largest city – Tokyo in Japan.

Australia

This is the world's smallest continent. It is surrounded by vast oceans. Most people live on islands, or along the coast.

FACT FILE

» **Land area:**
8.6 million sq km
(3.32 million sq miles)

» **Countries:** 4

» **Population:**
36 million

» **Largest city:**
Sydney

Uluru, Northern Territory

FACT FILE

» **Land area:**
30.37 million sq km
(11.73 million sq miles)

» **Countries:** 54

» **Population:**
1.21 billion

» **Largest city:**
Lagos

FACT FILE

» **Land area:**
14 million sq km
(5.41 million sq miles)

» **Countries:** 0

» **Population:** 4,000

» **Largest city:**
McMurdo Station

Masai Mara Reserve, Kenya

Africa

This is the second-largest continent and has the most countries. The world's longest river and the world's largest desert are in Africa.

Rural and urban

All over the world, people live in both rural and urban areas. In rural areas, there are few houses and lots of countryside. Many urban areas, such as towns and cities, are full of different buildings, and natural, green places are rarer. People often move between rural and urban areas.

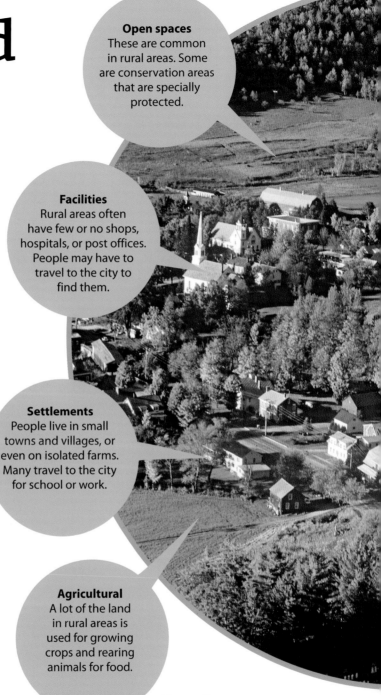

Open spaces
These are common in rural areas. Some are conservation areas that are specially protected.

Facilities
Rural areas often have few or no shops, hospitals, or post offices. People may have to travel to the city to find them.

Settlements
People live in small towns and villages, or even on isolated farms. Many travel to the city for school or work.

Agricultural
A lot of the land in rural areas is used for growing crops and rearing animals for food.

! WOW!
By 2030, **around 40 cities** will have populations of **over 10 million!**

Rural
Less people live in rural areas, so they are less built-up and have plenty of open, green spaces. Many people work on farms.

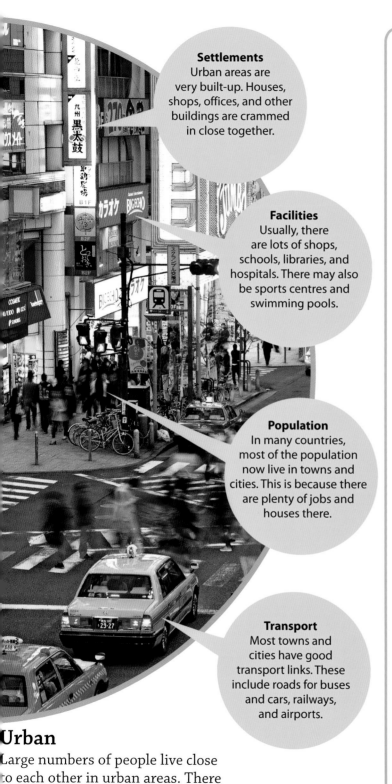

Settlements
Urban areas are very built-up. Houses, shops, offices, and other buildings are crammed in close together.

Facilities
Usually, there are lots of shops, schools, libraries, and hospitals. There may also be sports centres and swimming pools.

Population
In many countries, most of the population now live in towns and cities. This is because there are plenty of jobs and houses there.

Transport
Most towns and cities have good transport links. These include roads for buses and cars, railways, and airports.

Urban

Large numbers of people live close to each other in urban areas. There are many buildings and roads. People in cities do lots of different jobs.

Rural and urban populations

More and more people across the world are moving from rural to urban areas, where there are more jobs that are often better paid.

- Rural
- Urban

Europe
27% / 73%
Most people in Europe live in urban areas. The population of many cities is still growing.

Africa
60% / 40%
Here, more of the work is on farms. Therefore, most people remain in rural areas.

Asia
52% / 48%
The world's largest city, Tokyo, is in Asia. But just over half of all Asians live in rural areas.

South America
20% / 80%
The urban population here is expanding rapidly. Most people now live in cities.

Australia
11% / 89%
Some islands are still very rural, but most people live in cities, dotted along the coast.

North America
20% / 80%
Wide open spaces are common here, but few people live in them. Most prefer city life.

Mapping the world

Maps are a way of picturing the world. They can show a small area, such as your neighbourhood, or a very large area, such as the whole world. Different types of map show different things. Some show countries, while others may just show physical features, such as rivers and mountains.

Physical map

This type of map shows you the natural features in an area. These include mountains, volcanoes, rivers, lakes, seas, oceans, and deserts. Different colours and symbols are used to represent these features.

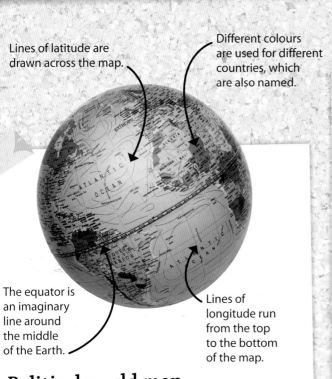

Lines of latitude are drawn across the map.

Different colours are used for different countries, which are also named.

The equator is an imaginary line around the middle of the Earth.

Lines of longitude run from the top to the bottom of the map.

Political world map

A political map shows you the countries of the world. You see where borders and cities are, including national capitals. Imaginary, numbered lines – the equator and lines of latitude and longitude – give you the exact position on Earth of places they pass through.

KEY

	Forest area
	Water
	Dry land
	Mountains
	River

Street map

This type of map shows where the streets and roads in a town or city are. It will also show bus stops, stations, schools, hospitals, parks, and other useful and important places.

Street and road names are clearly shown on the map.

Important buildings are featured and labelled.

KEY

M Metro station

Riverbus boarding point

Pedestrian street

i Information

A scale tells you how distances on the map correspond to real-life distances.

The compass symbol shows you where North, South, East, and West are on the map.

GPS map

This accurate, up-to-date map is created using digital technology. You can view GPS maps on your phone, tablet, or computer. They can tell you exactly where you are at any time.

Finish your journey here.

Start your journey here.

55

Meet the expert

Dr Amy Donovan works at the Department of Geography, King's College London in the UK. Her special interest is studying how science can help communities deal with the problems of living near active volcanoes. Dr Donovan also gives talks to schools and at science festivals, and writes for science journals.

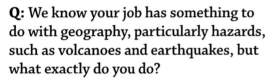

Q: We know your job has something to do with geography, particularly hazards, such as volcanoes and earthquakes, but what exactly do you do?

A: Mostly my work involves using scientific and other kinds of information to make decisions about land use and population management around active volcanoes. At the moment, I'm working on how different countries can work together to manage the effects of eruptions.

Q: What made you decide to study geography, and specialize in the problems caused by volcanoes and earthquakes?

A: My first degree was in English, but geography and geology had always been strong interests of mine, so I decided to study geoscience with the Open University. Then I did a MSc in geophysical hazards, and finally a PhD in volcanology!

Q: What is a typical day at work like for you?

A: I work in a university, so I spend a lot of time teaching. But I also have days when I'm out monitoring an active volcano, or gathering information from other scientists and civil protection officials. I might also spend time with people affected by volcanic activity to find out how they deal with the problems that brings. Other days may be spent in the laboratory, studying samples of

Special protective clothing is worn around volcanoes.

volcanic rock, or writing up my research, or attending a conference, or visiting schools and science fairs.

Q: Have you written any books or appeared on television?

A: I've been on television a few times, and sometimes I work as an adviser on programmes. I'm writing a book at the moment.

Q: What sort of equipment do you use?

A: At volcanic sites, I also use ultraviolet and infrared spectrometers to measure volcanic gases. I also use a lot of specialized software for mapping, and for analyzing the information that I gather from my research. In the laboratory, I use special instruments to measure the compositions of volcanic rocks.

Teamwork is important.

Q: How accurate is it possible to be when predicting an earthquake or a volcanic eruption?

A: It varies quite a lot. Earthquakes cannot be predicted, but we can identify areas that are at more risk than others.

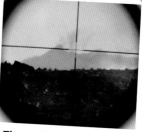
Through a spectrometer

For volcanoes, there are often signs that an eruption is likely to happen. However, we may not pick them up, as many volcanoes are not monitored closely, and signs that a volcano is about to become active can be hard to spot. But there have been opportunities to warn people and clear areas successfully before an eruption, such as with Mount Merapi in Indonesia in 2010.

Q: Is your job ever dangerous?

A: It can be! Volcanoes sometimes surprise you, and there have been times when I have had to move very quickly because of a sudden, unexpected increase in volcanic activity.

Q: What do you love most about your work?

A: I love my research. I love working with volcanologists and studying ways that people deal with the problems of living near a volcano. There's a lot to be learned, and it is exciting and satisfying to be involved in protecting a place from serious damage, or even destruction.

Q: What has been your most exciting experience so far?

A: I monitored the 2014–15 Holuhraun eruptions in Iceland. That was fantastic! We were in the Icelandic highlands, which are spectacular. It was the largest eruption there since 1783–84, so it was interesting scientifically, too.

Earth facts and figures

Our home planet is full of really amazing things. Here are some weird and wonderful facts you may not know about it!

6,000°C (10,830°F)

is the temperature at Earth's core. This is hotter than the surface of the Sun!

550

volcanoes have erupted on Earth's surface since records began. Around 60 are active every year.

It would take a whole year to walk around the Earth at its equator, without stopping.

9,000

This is the number of people the world's population grows by in one hour. That's the same as 25 plane-loads of passengers arriving on the planet every hour.

The oldest rocks the ocean floor a

380 billion years old.

...ussia is the **largest country**

...the world, covering 11.5 per cent of Earth's surface.

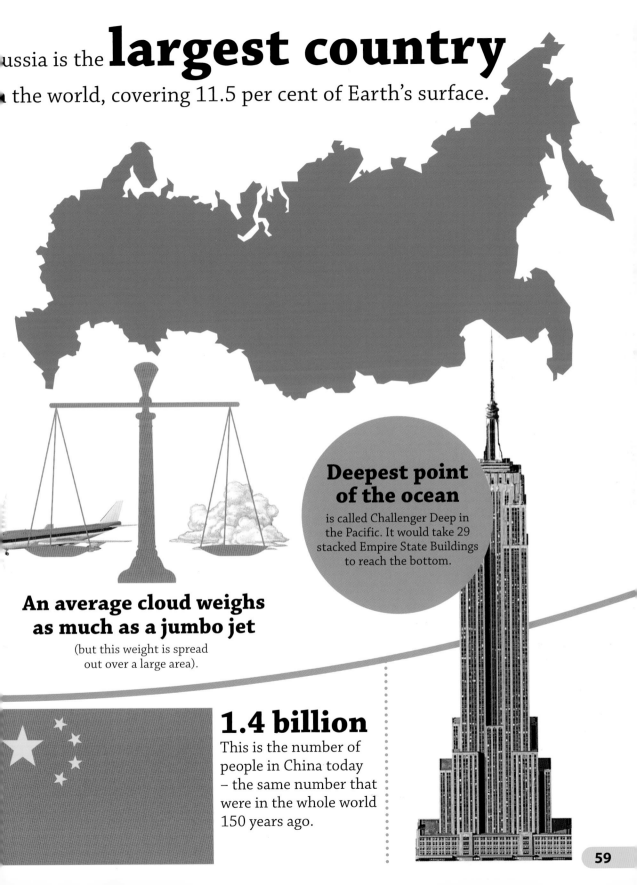

Deepest point of the ocean

is called Challenger Deep in the Pacific. It would take 29 stacked Empire State Buildings to reach the bottom.

An average cloud weighs as much as a jumbo jet

(but this weight is spread out over a large area).

1.4 billion

This is the number of people in China today – the same number that were in the whole world 150 years ago.

Glossary

Here are the meanings of some words that are useful for you to know when learning about the Earth.

atmosphere Thick layer of gases around the Earth that protect the planet from the burning rays of the Sun

biome Any main ecosystem on Earth with a particular vegetation and climate

blizzard A wind storm in which snow is blown quickly

cave A naturally occurring space inside a cliff or hillside

climate Weather patterns for a particular area

cloud Lots of very tiny water droplets and sometimes ice crystals

conservation Protecting an area on Earth

continent A large area of land, such as Asia

desert A very dry place on Earth. It has less than 25 cm (10 in) of rainfall every year

Earth The fifth-largest planet in our solar system

earthquake Movements in the Earth's crust that make the ground shake violently

equator An imaginary line that runs horizontally around the middle of Earth

erosion Breaking down of rock by weather or water

flooding When a river or the sea overflows and fills land with water

fresh water Water sources that are fresh and without sal

glacier Large mass of ice tha moves slowly down a slope

global positioning system (GPS) A radio navigation system that enables people to determine exact locations on Earth and obtain directions

grasslands A large, open area that is covered with grass and often used for grazing animal

habitat Natural home environment of an animal

heatwave A long period of time in which the weather is unusually hot

hurricane A storm with very fast and violent wind

lava Red-hot melted rock that flows out of a volcano when it erupts

map Representation of an area of land or sea, showing features such as borders, mountains, roads, and cities

Coral reef

mineral A group of chemicals forming a solid that occurs in nature, such as crystals

mountain A large landform that rises above the surrounding land, usually with a peak. A mountain is usually higher than a hill

polar Areas near the North and South Poles

pollution Waste that has been dumped in water, in the air, or on land. Pollution can have a negative effect on the environment

population The number of people living in a country or smaller area, such as a city or a town

rainforest An area with heavy rainfall, allowing lots of trees and other plants to grow. Many are also very hot

river A large body of water flowing in a channel to the sea, a lake, or another river

rock A group of minerals, forming a solid that is found underground or on the surface of the Earth

rural In the countryside. The opposite of urban

Atacama Desert, South America

season Yearly cycles of change that affect the weather, animals, and plants. The four seasons are spring, summer, autumn, and winter

seismograph A machine that measures earthquakes

snow Ice crystals that fall from clouds and stick together to form snowflakes

solar system The collection of eight planets that revolve around our Sun

storm Strong winds, between gale and hurricane force, of 103–121 km/h (64–75 mph)

tectonic plate Giant rocky plates that make up the Earth's crust

temperate An area or a climate with mild temperatures

tornado A thin spiral of air spinning at high speed around an area of extremely low air pressure. Wind speeds may be higher than 320 km/h (200 mph)

tropical An area or a climate with hot temperatures

tundra A cold, treeless area near the North and South Poles, where soil remains frozen for most of the year

urban A built-up area, such as a city or a large town. The opposite of rural

volcano Where hot magma breaks through the Earth's crust with great pressure

weathering The cracking of rocks by weather, plants, or chemicals

wetland Land made up of marshes or swamps

Index

Acknowledgements

The publisher would like to thank the following people for their assistance in the preparation of this book: Caroline Hunt for proofreading, Hilary Bird for the index, Ala Uddin for design assistance, and Dan Crisp for illustrations. The publishers would also like to thank Dr Amy Donovan for the "Meet the expert" interview.

The publisher would like to thank the following for their kind permission to reproduce their photographs:

(Key: a-above; b-below/bottom; c-centre; f-far; l-left; r-right; t-top)

2 iStockphoto.com: Bihaibo (crb). 3 CNES: ill. Pierre Carril (tr). Getty Images: Joe Carini (cb). 6 CNES: ill.Pierre Carril (cla). 7 Dreamstime.com: Andrey Armyagov (cr). 12 123RF.com: Tom Grundy (c). Alamy Stock Photo: Emmanuel LATTES (cb). 13 Depositphotos Inc: Simonwattsphoto (br). iStockphoto.com: Daniel Prudek (cla). 14 Dreamstime.com: Craig Hanson / Rssfhs (cra). 15 Alamy Stock Photo: Juergen Ritterbach (cr). Getty Images: Joe Carini (cra); Mario Vazquez (cl). 16 123RF.com: Destinacigdem (clb). 17 Getty Images: China Photos (cb). SuperStock: Dirk Bleyer / imagebroker (cla). 18 Depositphotos Inc: Jkraft5 (cl). Dreamstime.com: Galyna Andrushko (tc). 19 123RF.com: Danilo Forcellini (cb); Jejim (crb). Alamy Stock Photo: Colin Harris / era-images (c). Dreamstime.com: Patrick Poendl (cb/oases). FLPA: Colin Monteath, Hedgehog House / Minden Pictures (tc). 22 NASA: Jesse Allen / U.S. Geological Survey. Aerial photographs courtesy of the Hydrographic and Oceanographic Department, Japan Coast Guard. (c). 22-23 Dreamstime.com: David Carbo (t). 23 123RF. com: Brian Kinney (c). Dreamstime.com: Helen Hotson (tr). 24 123RF.com: Detanan (ca). 25 iStockphoto.com: Bihaibo (tc). SuperStock: Biosphoto (cb). 26-27 Science Photo Library: Bernhard Edmaier. 27 Imagelibrary India Pvt Ltd: Jaime Diaz (crb). 28 123RF.com: Joerg Hackemann (clb); Somchai Jongmeesuk (t). Dreamstime.com: Doughnuts64 (cb). 29 Alamy Stock Photo: Geogphoto (t). iStockphoto.com: MyImages_Micha (cb). 30 Dreamstime.com: George Burba (cb). 30-31 Alamy Stock Photo: Blickwinkel (t). 31 123RF.com: Mauro Rodrigues (crb); Valentyna Zhukova (clb). 32 Getty Images: Image Source (crb). 33 Getty Images: Stephen Alvarez (cra); FabioFilzi (crb). 34 123RF.com: NejroN (cr); Pongphan Ruengchai (clb). 35 123RF. com: Pavel Cheiko (tl); Juhani Viitanen (tr); Marina Vdovkina (bl). Depositphotos Inc: Znm666 (cr). 38 123RF.com: Marisha5 (tl). 38-39 123RF.com: Alexey Kamenskiy. 39 123RF.com: Wiml (tr); Montree Worasethakorn (tc). Getty Images: Yuri

Cortez (br). 40-41 123RF.com: Lilkar (c). 44 123RF.com: Morley Read (tr). Dreamstime.com: Andreanita (c). 45 Alamy Stock Photo: Norman Owen Tomalin (crb). Dreamstime.com: Marcovarro (cl). 47 123RF.com: Tobkatrina (tc/canyon). Depositphotos Inc: Naticastillog (tr). Dreamstime.com: Aitor Muñoz Muñoz (tc). 48 123RF.com: Sun_Rise (cl). 49 Dorling Kindersley: Natural History Museum, London (cr). Dreamstime.com: Andrew Barker (tr). 50 123RF.com: Bernard Bodo (ca). iStockphoto. com: JohnnyLye (c). 50-51 iStockphoto.com: RichLindie (b). 51 123RF.com: Feiyuwzhangjie (ca); Vit Kovalcik (cla). Dreamstime.com: Joshua Cortopassi (cr). 53 123RF.com: Visions of America LLC (r). Getty Images: Oleksiy Maksymenko (l). 54-55 Depositphotos Inc: Delpieroo (b). 56-57 Dr Amy Donovan: (All). 60 123RF.com: Brian Kinney (bl). Getty Images: Joe Carini (tl). 61 Depositphotos Inc: jkraft5 (tr). 62 123RF.com: Tobkatrina (tl). 64 Alamy Stock Photo: Blickwinkel (tl)

Cover images: Front: 123RF.com: 1xpert l, NejroN cr; CNES: ill.Pierre Carril fcra; Back: 123RF. com: Somchai Jongmeesuk clb; Dorling Kindersley: Natural History Museum, London c Dreamstime.com: Mtoumbev tl; Spine: 123RF. com: 1xpert b; Front Flap: 123RF.com: Jejim b; Alamy Stock Photo: Blickwinkel tr; Depositphotos Inc: Znm666 cb; Imagelibrary India Pvt Ltd: Jaime Diaz bl; iStockphoto.com: MyImages_Micha cla; Back Flap: iStockphoto. com: Naumoid tc; NASA: cb

All other images © Dorling Kindersley
For further information see:
www.dkimages.com

My Findout facts

··

··

··

··

··

··

··

··

··

··

··

··

··

··

··

··

Famous explorers

Pytheas

Exploration

Date: 4th century BCE

This Ancient Greek explorer sailed into the seas of northern Europe, reaching Scandinavia. He was the first person to report about the midnight sun, polar ice, and auroras.

Zhang Qian

Exploration

Date: 2nd century BCE

Zhang Qian opened a new route from China to the West through central Asia. This became known as the Silk Road and was used by merchants.

Jeanne Baret

Exploration

Date: 1766 – 1769

Baret was the first woman to sail around the world. She assisted the expedition's botanist. To be allowed on the voyage, she had to dress as a young boy.